I0693274

HI, I'M TOMMY! I LOVE PLAYING WITH
MY TOYS AND SPLASHING IN PUDDLES.
ADVENTURE IS MY MIDDLE NAME--
WELL, EXCEPT WHEN IT'S TIME TO EAT...

SOME FOODS FEEL STRANGE.

BANANAS ARE SQUISHY,

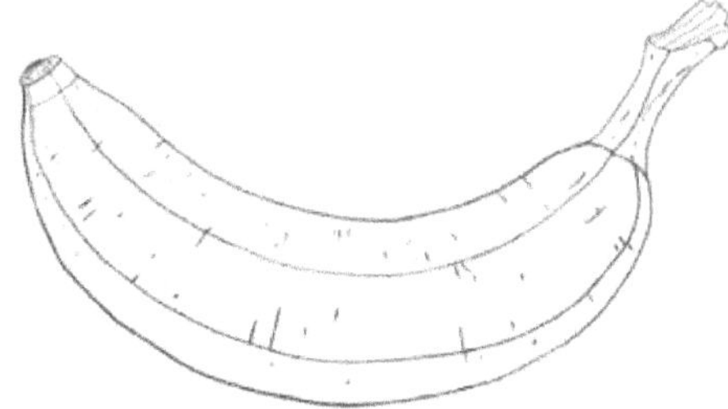

CARROTS ARE CRUNCHY,

SPAGHETTI'S SO wild!

THEY MAKE ME FEEL ICKY, JUST NOT MY STYLE.

ONE DAY, MOM BRINGS ME A NEW PLATE.
"THIS IS YOUR ADVENTURE PLATE, TOMMY."
SHE SAYS WITH A SMILE.
"WE'RE GOING ON AN ADVENTURE
WITH NEW FOODS TO TRY,
SO LET'S MAKE IT WORTHWHILE!"

THE PLATE HAS LITTLE SPOTS FOR EACH FOOD,
SOME ARE *SOFT*, SOME *CRUNCHY*, SOME *SMOOTH*.
"YOU CAN START WHEREVER YOU WANT,"
MOM ENCOURAGES ME GENTLY.

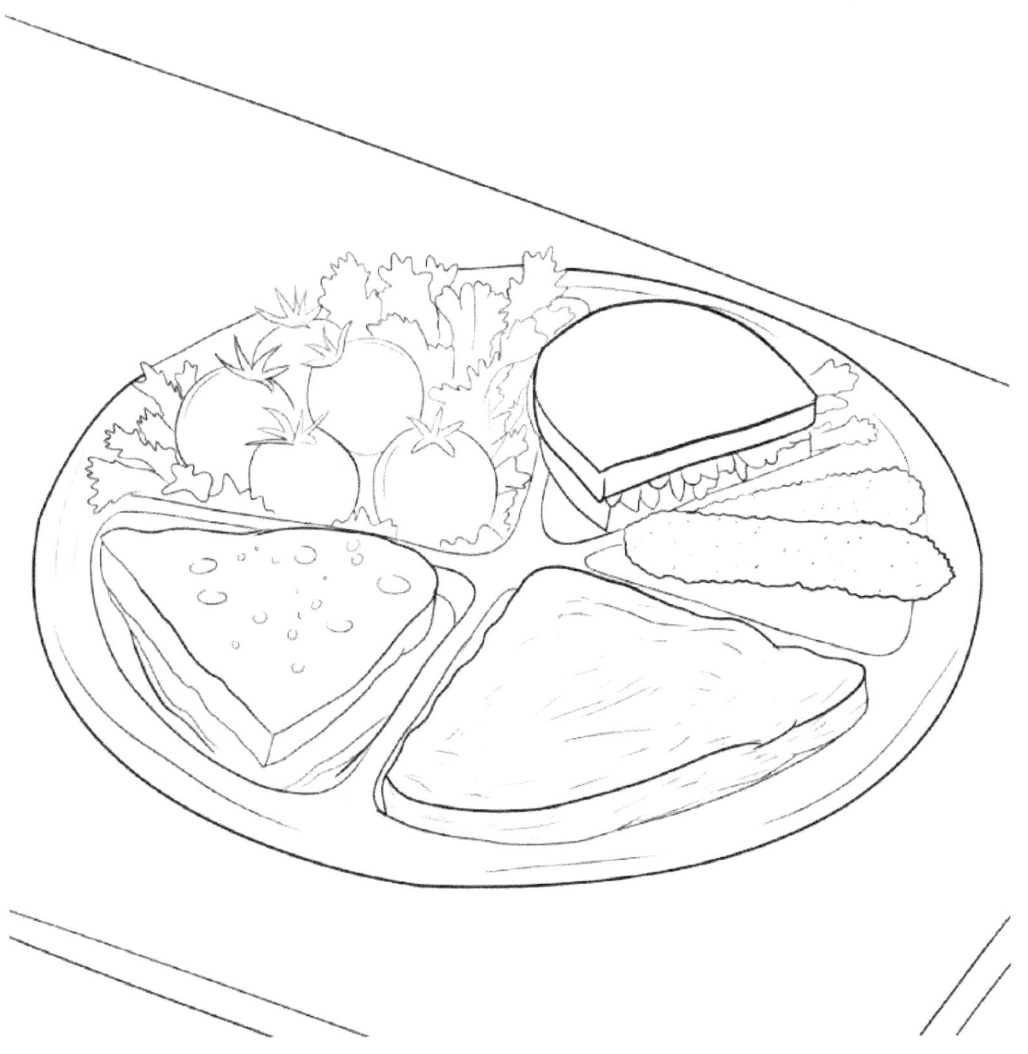

I'M A BIT NERVOUS, BUT I DO LOVE A GOOD QUEST.
I DECIDED TO START WITH THE YOGURT- IT'S SMOOTH AND LOOKS BEST.

I DIP MY SPOON IN AND TAKE A TINY TASTE.
"MMM, THAT'S NOT BAD AT ALL! THIS ADVENTURE HAS STARTED OFF GREAT!"

NEXT, I TRY A CRUNCHY CRACKER.
AT FIRST, THE SOUND MAKES MY EARS TWITCH
BUT THEN I REALIZED IT'S JUST LIKE MY BLOCKS!
"CRUNCHY CAN BE FUN! WHAT A COOL THOUGHT SWITCH!"

THEN THERE'S AVOCADO. GREEN AND MUSHY,
IT'S SQUISHY AND SOFT- IT FEELS KIND OF FUNNY.
I TAKE A DEEP BREATH, POP IT IN MY MOUTH.

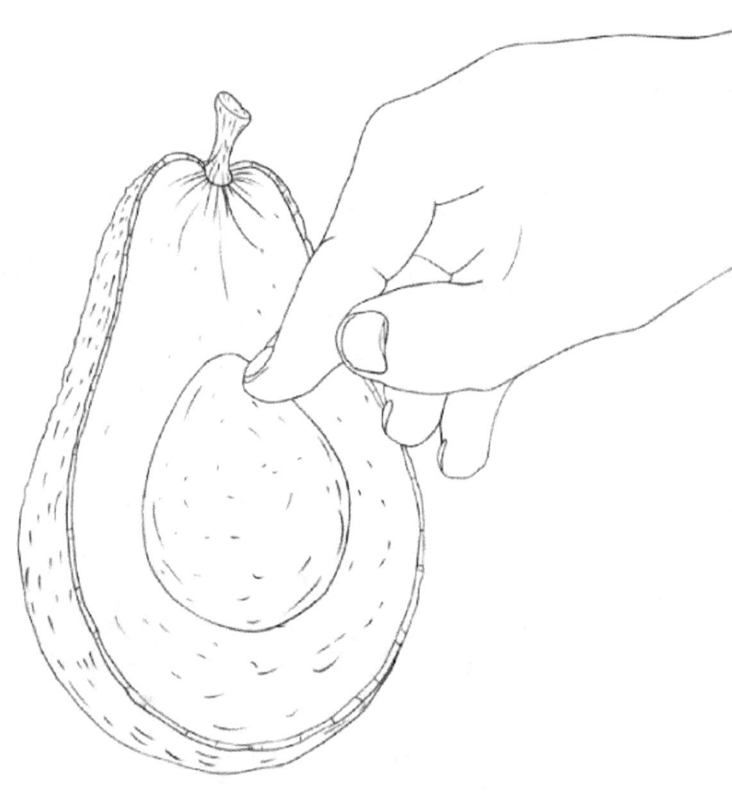

YUCK! IT'S SO GROSS, I WANT TO SPIT IT OUT!

EVERY NEW TASTE FEELS LIKE A SURPRISE.
SOME MAKE ME SMILE, OTHERS MAKE ME SIGH,
BUT TRYING EACH NEW FOOD MAKES ME FEEL BRAVER INSIDE.

MOM SAYS, "IT'S OKAY TO NOT LIKE EVERYTHING.
SOME THINGS YOU MAY LOVE, AND SOME YOU MAY HATE.
THE IMPORTANT THING IS TRYING. YOU'RE DOING GREAT!"

I'M SO PROUD OF MYSELF FOR BEING BRAVE
AND TRYING NEW THINGS!

"HEY MOM, CAN I TRY SOMETHING NEW AGAIN TOMORROW?"

"OF COURSE, HONEY! WE'LL HAVE MORE FUN
AND NEW THINGS TO EXPLORE!"

"GOODNIGHT, ADVENTURE PLATE," I WHISPER,
READY FOR SWEET DREAMS AND A TASTY ADVENTURE!

AS I DRIFT OFF TO SLEEP, MY HEART FEELS SO LIGHT,
I THINK ABOUT ALL THE YUMMY FOODS WAITING IN SIGHT.

IN MY DREAMS, I EXPLORE
TASTY ADVENTURES GALORE.

"FOOD ISN'T SO SCARY AFTER ALL," I SMILE WITH DELIGHT.
ADVENTURE IS EVERYWHERE, EVEN IN A TINY BITE!

Everday With Differences

Everyday With Differences is a heartfelt children's book series that shines a gentle, authentic light on the everyday lives of kids with disabilities. From big challenges to seemingly small moments, each story unfolds from the perspective of a child, capturing their unique experiences and the relatable ups and downs of daily life. Through the eyes of these young characters, readers discover the courage, joy, and resilience that make each day an adventure. Adding to the series' authenticity, every book is illustrated by talented disabled artists, bringing these stories to life with warmth and depth. Whether it's learning to try new foods, handling sensory overload, finding alternative ways to communicate, or managing tics, each book highlights the beauty of diversity and the power of self-expression in an accessible and compassionate way.

Do you have a disability that you want featured in an Everyday With Differences book?

Send an email to EverydayWithDifferences@gmail.com

Tell me what the medical diagnosis is and a little bit about it.

What are the advantages and disadvantages of living with

the disability. Is there anything specific that you would

like for the book to feature?

Are you an artist with a disability and want to illustrate an Everyday With Differences book?

The books will proudly state that they were illustrated by artists with disabilities, celebrating their incredible perspectives and creativity.

How to enter:
Submit a picture in the style you envision for illustrating the book (it does not need to be a new picture).
Write a paragraph about yourself and explain why you'd be perfect for illustrating a book in this series.

What's in it for you?
Full credit and royalties for every book sold
A free copy of every book in the series, including future releases.

The contest is ongoing, so you can reapply every month with different artwork. This is a wonderful chance to showcase your talent and contribute to a meaningful project that advocates for awareness and inclusion.

I can't wait to see your amazing artwork and share these stories with the world through your eyes!

To submit your entry, email all required information to EverydayWithDifferences@gmail.com

Lets make a difference together!

Tommy's Tasty Challenge

Have a taste of something:

- ☐ Crunchy
- ☐ Creamy
- ☐ Fluffy
- ☐ Squishy
- ☐ Stringy
- ☐ Gummy
- ☐ Sticky
- ☐ Juicy
- ☐ Crumbly
- ☐ Fizzy
- ☐ Grainy
- ☐ Sweet
- ☐ Salty
- ☐ Savory
- ☐ Sour
- ☐ Bitter
- ☐ Spicy
- ☐ Tangy
- ☐ Black
- ☐ Brown
- ☐ White
- ☐ Red
- ☐ Orange
- ☐ Yellow
- ☐ Green
- ☐ Blue
- ☐ Purple
- ☐ Pink

Which was your favorite?

Which was your least favorite?

My Food Adventure Journal

Date:

Food Tried:

What I liked:

What I didn't like:

How I felt after trying it:

Date:

Food Tried:

What I liked:

What I didn't like:

How I felt after trying it:

Date:

Food Tried:

What I liked:

What I didn't like:

How I felt after trying it:

My Food Adventure Journal

Date:

Food Tried:

What I liked:

What I didn't like:

How I felt after trying it:

Date:

Food Tried:

What I liked:

What I didn't like:

How I felt after trying it:

Date:

Food Tried:

What I liked:

What I didn't like:

How I felt after trying it:

Color your own adventure plate

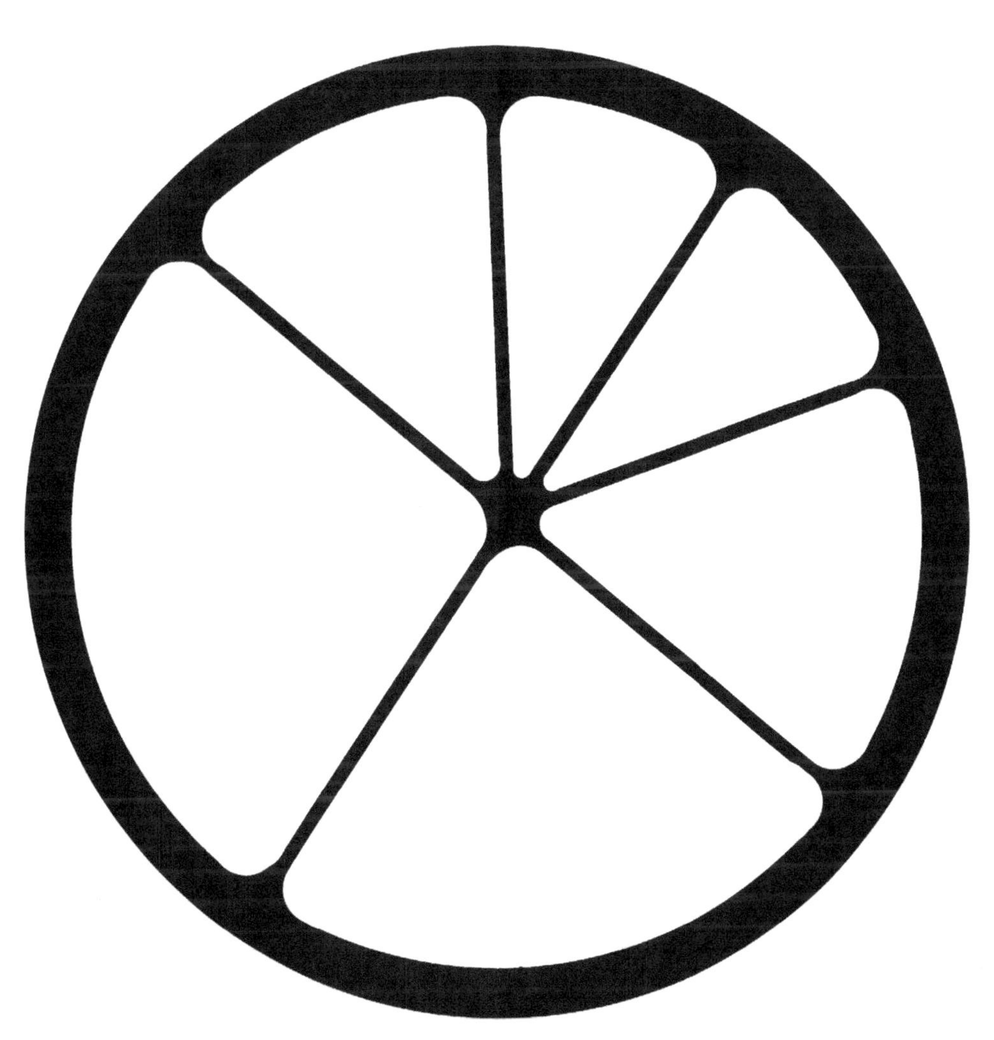